COLLEGE TOWN

COLLEGE TOWN

MICHAEL MILLER

TEBOT BACH • HUNTINGTON BEACH • CALIFORNIA • 2010

Cover painting by Josh Naehu-Reyes
Design, layout by Melanie Matheson, Rolling Rhino Communications

ISBN 13:   978-1-893670-46-4
ISBN 10:   1-893670-46-5

Library of Congress Control Number: 2009941521

A Tebot Bach book

Tebot Bach, Welsh for little teapot, is A Nonprofit Public Benefit Corporation
which sponsors workshops, forums, lectures, and publications. Tebot Bach
books are distributed by Small Press Distribution, Armadillo and Ingram.

The Tebot Bach Mission: Advancing Literacy, Strengthening Community,
and transforming life experiences with the power of poetry through readings,
workshops, and publicatons.

This book is made possible by a grant from The San Diego Foundation
Steven R. and Lera B. Smith Fund at the recommendation of Lera Smith.

www.tebotbach.org

CONTENTS

FOREWORD

Poetry needs Michael Miller. Indeed, anyone able to write a power-fully spare pair of lines like "He tells himself, *Nothing but a woman,* / tells himself, *We scavenge together*" rewards the reader and honors the craft. The power of Miller's writing is in his imagery, syntactical skills, and ability to capture the *now* of the experiential terrain. And although the image, the bright, focused *instant*, is never more than a line or two away, such moments of sound and sense, for ear and eye—"ocean breeze and the crash of the fountain"—are certain to surprise and excite.

Equally powerful is Miller's evocative use of color: the "girls in mas-cara / who glint like fireflies in the yellow lamps," or the stretch of a woman's communique "finger / polished red half sober texting." In short, these are powerful *photographs*; and among them also are difficult, though perfected, motion images like new babies' "swirling eyes" or the imagistic gem caught in "Coffee Shop" where a girl's dress scatters dust as she "twirls her shape." These are pictures that truly put the reader *there*, and when linked by lines communing sense and sound such as "cards telling stories / of when this town was dust, when everyone was hungry," Miller's writing is unsurpassed, and so is his wordplay.

The great strength of Miller's poetry also derives from syntactical rep-etition, which he energetically employs. In "Cold Water," the liquid "runs down her throat / *like hands* / running down the length of her clothes / *like feet* / running down the stairs" [my italics]. Elsewhere, the lines, frenetic at Miller's bidding, come to rest as the characters "sleep abundant on the dust of tombs" ("Like a Cathedral"). This quick-soft alternation, more than not, is essential, because many writers—too calm, too reflective and too tranquil—simply rest at the center of the poem (as in narrative) or stand to the side, leaving the reader an all too passive bystander.

In Miller's writing, there is, further, the quiet expectation of exultant or dramatic play. In "Thief After Dark," an elegy of longing and theft of heart, the "thief" therein turns his back, at last, to his intended amorous victim and finally ponders that there's "nothing left to steal." Indeed, throughout Miller's work, the lines are robust, stimulating and full of the poetic moment, as when a woman drowses in the "thick white air" ("Cold Water"), or when Miller's waitress in the final poem ("Blues Man") "shuts out the light / unscarred / and heads for the dead of home."

Given the craft, talent and imagination inherent in Miller's work, each of us would do well to emulate his focus, drive and passion for the word. In the sometime emptiness and estrangement of these days, we find poignancy, hope, and consolation within these poems.

—LEE MALLORY
NEWPORT BEACH

I.

ON THE TOWN

I am tall, but not ever so tall as the city at night.

—Kate Buckley

NIGHT COMPANION

Through a back window on a dead stone street,
she crawls in unnoticed.
The painted apostles on the wall,
which followed her feet twelve hours ago,
disappeared at dusk.
Now the city lies down to rest,
while she comes up to be a silhouette
in a second-story room.

I sit back with my eyes half-open,
not really seeing a thing.
She lets her jacket drop by the bed
and with a nervous smile
offers me a stick of incense
and the last box of matches she could find.
I haven't moved in at least an hour.
The smoke plays games
with the evening sky,
wrapping around the lines of trees
like a pair of soft gray healing hands.

Faceless in the dark, we are nothing but promise.
Her mouth reshapes me. The day falls behind.
As midnight nears in a cool dark cloud,
she lowers her head to the pillow and breathes.
I lie sleepless with my arm across her,
the god of the city now, and watch her dream.

COLLEGE TOWN

In a city awake on tea and subtitles,
the freshman boys fight off sleep
to hear a bluesman sing at the corner club,
his foot tapping and hoarse voice wailing

about fleeing the river hounds; and all the faces
look warm and dry here, the Lost Boys of Sudan
sheltered behind glass and glowing
on the art-house cinema, the neon sign

of the conquistador blinking over the nightclub
with his rifle drawn (the children of the Aztecs
on the sidewalk below seeking wristbands cool
in their pressed silk collars) — here the bus shakes

to a stop every hour, the doors snapping open
and the couples pass (consummated)
through ocean breeze and the crash of the fountain
in search of a drink — the girls in mascara

who glint like fireflies in the yellow lamps,
the one who breaks from the line at the tavern
and ducks into the gallery, past
the corner magician and the swirling eyes

of new babies, stands wet by the glare
of the bootleggers brutal and handsome under
their shaded brims in a portrait
in the hall, the newspapers cheering New Deal

and the trays of Cabernet in back (a finger
polished red half sober texting
about *free food, gallery show, what time
do u get off wk)* — the kisses stolen

over floodlights and the donation box
overflowing by ten, the eyes of migrants
that lust from photographs, the cards telling stories
of when this town was dust, when everyone was hungry.

THE CHIEF

Somewhere that weekend the chief turned thirty.
They pooled their dollars for a case of beer,
then, after lingering,
walked the narrow stairway to his door,
too frail to face the pole dancers.

He hushed them as they came inside,
nodding to the woman on his bed.
One of them stood apart in the kitchen
smelling her scent along the carpet
and left, finding no one to rescue.

The rest stayed, laughing off the day shift,
turning around their Indians caps.
One made jokes about the casinos;
another danced before the spirits
for a clean job, a safer route home.

Only the youngest one stayed sober,
rummaging through the bedroom drawers
for what was left of the Trail of Tears,
practicing his stoic face in the glass,
clutching the torn moccasins.

ROSES

Go to her milk-bottle street
past the torn line of billboards,
climb the tease of stairs,
the overture of railings
where the roses breathe jubilation
over the sad chime of arcades,

where buses move the day from stop to stop,
shrug at evening,
answer *yes* to your walking shoes.
You step off at her doorway,
breathing,

tap against her crooked window.
The locks tremble, ease you inside.
She offers you a wash of roses,
a bed within her tightening walls,
the ashes that she takes from you
as her knuckles part your hair.

The red petals spread out in her window
like spring, a source behind the railing.
Go to her when the vegetation dies.

COLD WATER

cold water
runs down her throat
like hands
running down the length of her clothes
like feet
running down the stairs
at the end of an endless working day
miles away
from her room overlooking the street
and the elevator rising
up stories of electricity
copper wire and ice machines
pulsing inside the walls
she lies
absent from the hall
outside
back straight against a narrow bed
with a cold glass pressed to her head
and lips
catching the ends of her hair
too innocent to be awake
in the space between the thick white air
and the shaking of her skin
passengers on the subway
dream of fountains outside the window
drifters in the park
walk on wells hidden deep below
she sits
found
in a hot dry room
with water running down her throat
and my hands
cold out of the icebox
touching her like a stethoscope

HOST

Before he passes the reefers out,
he checks himself in the mirror —
black jacket with the collar pressed,
hair parted,
skin like sand.
When he tore the cuff link on his right,
he lit her cigarette with his left,
knowing that when the hour was late,
she would never let herself be drugged
by a less than perfect hand.

WOMAN IN THE HEIGHTS

You must love me
if you know the way a white oak spreads
behind stoic black gates, the glow of street lamps
catching naked sinews and carved immaculate steel,
the rails fusing with fingertips of vines —
if you know the swallow,
the airtightness of curtains
that draw a house back from fluid evening
the way fears of hunger
and a sleek briefcase drew me racing
surrendering north of the freeway —
the pulse, the beating of identical driveways
with eaves stretched silent behind the lawns.

Take the highway past tents and infirmaries,
the love notes scrawled on the sides of locomotives;
pass through the sleeping plazas,
the square white buildings cut out of clouds
and the hospital sign
that looms painlessly over the valley;
carry your features, your face and arms
that roamed through miles
of unbelievable sun,
to my doorstep beaming with a single porch light.
Flicker through the windows of supermarkets,
the indifferent eyes of policemen and cameras.

You alone know the majesty of railings,
how a fountain surges in place all night
and every ripple is necessary.
The streets here bend around hedges and electric wire,
curving toward perfection, never finding a sphere.

Come be an excavator, bring your lantern and brush
and dust every fingerprint, every sign of living.
Knock three times and wait for the curtains
to darken. Lie when I ask your name.

PATROLMAN SPEAKS

When I was a child
my father drove me
past the all-night cafes
where patrol cars shine,

the black-and-whites
lined under the low trees,
the glow of ceiling lights
catching the vines

on the curving road.
The jukebox played
in the back through laughter;
two waitresses danced

with the smallest one,
their bodies swaying
in a blue suit and dresses.
My father glanced

at the dashboard and drove.
I gazed at the wheels
that perched under sirens
in the fading brush

like rides at a carnival,
a beckoning field
with the gates unlocked,
all the doors free to touch.

ARMISTICE

The general came to casino row last night,
blessing the boats with his trigger finger
and signing peace to the riverside,
starry-eyed, watching the planes take flight,
free and silver against the dome.

Magic left his soldier clothes behind.
He walked with the silence of a priest
and lit his cigarettes like a spy,
with his card, waving, buying kegs of wine
for the refugees in cool black clothes.

A new kind of mother's milk ran through town
that evening. The lamps made love to faces
stooped at the bar; slot machines sounded
in windows, an invitation sent down
to the hangers-on. The general strode

past cracks into the shine of the city square
where the banners hung, shouting armistice;
the children of casualties lined the stairs,
dollars in pockets, nations in their hair
and skin. None of them blinked or spoke

as he climbed the steps, the glint of wire in his bones,
asking the women the way to church
so he could set his hand on a soul
carved out and polished. They sent him, alone,
as the troop melted in pace behind.

In the loft, the drifters woke to neon on shades.
One prayed, took his pulse. One rose to meet
the procession, dressed, threw open the drapes
and stood with his scars at the windowpane,
charmed by the brush of feet on stone.

Below him, the watchmen sat with their radios on,
buzzing with rage, the voices cracking
unanswered. The second hands ticked toward dawn.
But the general beckoned and sent his bronze
through the crowd, his dog tags glistening cold.

We tracked him, the two of us, and thanked him with smiles,
then left when he vanished. Our skin still shook.
We drifted home to the warm high rise,
awake and poor another Saturday night,
and retreated to our separate rooms.

II.

SUNRISE

At the counter sit the broken down
with real stories to tell.

—Michael Ubaldini

COFFEE SHOP

In a coffee shop by the docks, Norah Jones
is singing on a portable radio. No one listens.
The owner boils water and hands a rag
to the girl with the stutter — who doesn't work there —

and lets her wipe down the tables. They half-listen
as the rain drizzles and the man at the counter
rambles about the garage, though he doesn't work there
anymore, and how he stopped believing in God

when the Red Sox went all the way. The counter
fills with men from the shelter. *Another lost morning,*
the owner mutters, then swallows, thanks God
for the usual blessings: softcore and cigarettes,

the same beaten crowd that comes every morning
and spends what it has to spend. The girl
finishes the tables now, shakes the ends of cigarettes
out of the ashtrays. The foreman saunters in

with his newspaper wet, hands his coat to the girl
(who hangs it on the rack, glad to be of use)
and slumps by the radio. The voice saunters in
over bass and piano, a cool note of blue

as thunder roars outside. Keen to be of use,
he orders coffee around, turns the radio up high
and beckons the girl to dance. Her blue
dress scatters dust as he twirls her shape

by the clouds on the window, the notes surging high
and the voice cracking through static, Norah Jones
ravaged and beautiful like all of them. By the shape
of the docks under rain, they dance happy in rags.

THE ACTIVISTS

He learns to crave her body
reminding himself
that it's impermanent.
He's counted her wounds —
the mark on her shoulder the picket sign left
after months of trudging down the stairs
to the latest demonstration,
the rasp in her voice from shouting at traffic,
the way her throat quivers
when she bolts the food
they bought with the part of their paychecks
they were willing to spare.
Swallowing hunger himself,

he hangs a bag by the carport
and casts his thin arms against it, fearless.
At night, he lies awake with her
on a secondhand mattress, the blinds open,
facing the stars and her poster of Schindler
and listens — never answering —
while she asks
if they would have stood to block the cattle cars.
She tells him love is incitement.
He believes her. Their weekends wind

through cold showers and pipes with the Navajos,
hours awake past midnight on caffeine
with petitions drafted on the table,
her heirlooms, then his
surrendered on the dealer's counter
and turned into cash for the clinics in Sudan.
She leaves for work

and he digs her out of the hamper,
inhales the smell of her
from straps, shirts, her sweatband from jogging.
The early days still haunt him.
Alone in the kitchen,
he replays the First Communion,
high school in the limousine,
the road trips with his grandfather in Texas
when he waved his hand by the window
and pictured empires on the plains.
He holds his eyes steady now,

cool as a sniper, faces down the trucks
that roll looming off the factory farms,
the skyline thick with gas station globes,
savors the hardness of her as she bends
sunburned at the sink in the evening,
the light bulb fading and cans on the stove.
He tells himself, *Nothing but a woman,*
tells himself, *We scavenge together.*

BIRTH

This is
the rush of days in fast forward,
a soundless churn of steam on the kettle,
the sun snared in a mobile making kaleidoscopes on the upstairs wall,
sweat on torn slippers racing up the banister,
the roots of sermons and night confessions piercing through a white plastic
   monitor,
excitement of chatter over morning newspapers with coffee rings staining the
   dictator's face,
steam in clouds hiding Sunday from the mirror,
circle of bloodlines mixed race in the morning pressing frail hands to
   ancestors' fingers,
the moon on the mobile through an alabaster window turning stars into mystic
   ships and tiny men,
invisible telephones ringing unanswered,
the fierce faces of lions and tigers stuffed and tamed on the bedroom shelf,
fire trucks on the floor without sirens,
tableau of mother father and child in a crooked living room through frayed tree
   branches,
trinity of soldiers gazing at the dawn burning circles on winter driveways,
everyone steadfast too strong to fall.

LIKE A CATHEDRAL

Like a cathedral,
she is stone and echo,
warm sanctuary for the hands and mouth
with wooden angels in the corners
missing eyes.

She and I slip in, drop our coins
in the battered collection plate on the table.
The pews are empty.
We are country travelers,
our shoes torn from stepping on brambles
and the rocks on the path outside.

I brush my mouth across her
and kiss the markers of saints,
the forgotten, stillborn.
Each brick an eternity.
The doors in back fade into corridors,
darkened by centuries, sculpted by hands.

Set every candle on the altar burning.
Churn the water in the baptism tub.

Her face is stained glass and rusted jewels.
Invaders now,
we ransack for treasure,
sleep abundant on the dust of tombs.

I WENT INTO THE DESERT TO FIND MY LOVE

I went into the desert to find my love
because I was tired of waiting for the cold,
stationed at evening, looking through curtain folds
to picture the chill of a hand without a glove;
I went to see the canyon, where rocks shoved
against each other, and jagged mountains rolled
up to the aching sun, as fierce and old
as the planes of heaven my mind had seen above.
Across the valley where nothing new could thrive,
I searched the lines of strangers, cracked and brown,
for a weathered look of joy. I had survived
alone long enough to lay my visions down,
and touch the face of deliverance, alive,
in the shabby ruins of a country town.

SOPRANO

The soprano who sings
on this record player
and makes the hour seem twice as slow
passed away a long time ago
and doesn't remember recording this song.

They said she was hungry, slept too little,
wandered lonely by the docks at night.
The man from the chapel spreads out his bride
on the covers,
laughs as his palms give chase.

She laughs with him, maneuvers his fingers
down her chest, hips tightening.
He tears her lace
to the rhythm of violins, a piercing note
with piano frozen on an acetate.

They listen, giddy, as she gropes for heaven.
Her invisible hand strokes the microphone.
Still flesh, the three of them break for air,
then spread out their lungs again, ecstatic
like spirits treading the atmosphere.

THIEF AFTER DARK

When I slipped in before daybreak,
you were already in bed,
half-undressed
and sleeping on my side.
I didn't say a word
as I watched you through the half-closed door.
I thought I might have been a thief.

The only man standing awake
in a silent house along the coast
with the window open two rooms down
as if the lock had been picked.
No one saw me
as I stepped out of the shadows
in my night coat and gloves,
the darkest figure to pass through here
without setting off the alarm.

You lay flat on your back
with your arms beside your head,
sweat cooling in drops
on the curve of your neck.
If I had been a thief,
slipping out before the dawn,
I never would have seen you any other way,
not even the next morning
when you stared into the mirror
looking for some trace of moonlight
in the lines below your eyes
and I sat with my back turned to you
and nothing left to steal.

DECEMBER

I want to be a passenger
in your car again
and shut my eyes
while you sit at the wheel,

awake and assured
in your own private world,
seeing all the lines
on the road ahead,

down a long stretch
of empty highway
without any other
faces in sight.

I want to be a passenger
in your car again
and put my life back
in your hands.

III.

THE WEEK AFTER SEPT. 11

We have always made strangers out of ourselves
by loving others.

—Elena Karina Byrne

THE NURSE

Death became beautiful to me that week.
I rose at dawn to greet it,
wore it like a silk around my shoulders.
I thrilled at the sight of the flowers sinking
in the infested garden below my window,
the withered petals drooping toward the pavement
like old men on canes.

The woman on the television said war was cyclical.
I craved cycles too,
the swarm of insects in the alley
and the sun rising an inch at a time
on the chipped apartment sign
reading *Paradise Villas*.
I memorized the rhythms of the busker
camping out each morning at six,
the sex offender turning his single lamp on
and never lifting the shades.

My daughter woke in tears,
rummaged through the top shelf of the closet
for the dolls she'd put away years ago.
My husband left for work
and tripped each time over the bent bottom step.
I divorced them both,
wandered downtown through the skeleton fields,
passed faces of people and boarded-up buildings,
crumbling, smiling.

Noon took me weightless to an elevator,
a white tile floor and syringes,
my shift for the afternoon.
The woman on the television lectured me,
said I was to blame for Palestine.
My feet glided.
I took the wrists of nuns

and the wrists of dockworkers with tattoos,
counted the seconds as their blood filled plastic.

At midnight, the rest of the block still
and the street lamp shorted out, I sought life.
I plunged back into the leaf-strewn pool,
drank in the moon —
that bright dancing scavenger —
as she glinted over the telephone lines,
tasted the muggy September air
that fused the ground with secretive rain.
The neighbors' open window served as watchdog.
My husband's gun slept by the pillow inside.

I sank below and felt water pulling me,
pulling me back from my shadow life
on the surface,
my temporary face and name
and the apartment where I sleepwalked through the day
with mice in the kitchen
and the television on all the time,

back into wetness,
the baptismal font and the womb,
the first few breaks of consciousness.
I sank until oxygen forced me again
to surge to the light
and survive.

THE STEPSON

What I remember is Wednesday
my brother got up in the dark
unwrapped the BB gun
from the dirty towel we kept it in
filled his canteen with two shots of bourbon
dug five bottles out of the trash
and lined them
on the fence outside

our stepfather's leather jacket
hanging too big for his shoulders
his arm white knuckled
fighting to hold the barrel steady —
he took a swig of the bourbon
and said *We're all gonna get recruited*
nicked each bottle
then ran inside
when the lady upstairs turned her light on
and I stood on the lawn
jacket over my pajamas
squeezed a shadow trigger
and smashed all five —
that was the morning
eleven years old
I taught myself how to shoot.

Next I remember
is the locker room at school
the Lazyboys crowded around Juan in the corner
as he flashed the box cutter
he brought from home
and snuck in his pocket past the guard
(daring all of them to touch it
and leave their fingerprints)
the flagpole at noon
when the choir girls sang God Bless America
and the principal said tomorrow
was on our shoulders —

the flag waving
over hooded shirts
and no one looking anyone in the eye.

After that was murmurs
low voices through the walls at home
my mother on the phone
whispering to her mother in Spanish
the TV on
and dinner forgotten in the oven —
my stepfather bent on the couch with a cigarette
and grumbling that Bush
had fucked us over again —
myself in the bathroom mirror
red faced from another slam to the locker
flexing what I had
dropping for pushups
and telling myself I'd shove back next time.

They draft the white kids last
my brother said
and Friday afternoon
we set ourselves training—
six of us hungry on the playground
bumping fists
and swearing we'd enlist when we turned eighteen.
Julio called Navy
and held his breath in the deep end after school
until the lifeguard pulled him out choking.
Enrique called Marines
and laid into the taggers going home.
I called sniper

and went guessing the terrorists —
the fat man next door
I heard through the wall
when he yelled at his wife to pour him whiskey
the pervert across the balcony
who never talked and had his mug online
the women in scarves
who prayed on the sidewalk

when the mosque burned on the corner Sunday
their backs turned and the horns going by.
You were eleven once too.
I sat at the window
and pictured them all wearing bombs and wire.

THE DEALER

The woman upstairs,
the one who kept the chain on
when she answered the door that summer,
handed me a prayer angel,
kissed me on the cheek
and invited me to kneel
in a circle in her living room,
ten strangers packed between the couch and stereo,
holding hands and trusted not to rob her
when she bowed and shut her eyes.

We are all reborn this week, she said.
I watched myself watch them in the glass,
my clothes a carpenter's,
skin smooth with light.
When they called for our names,
I was Pablo,
the shy boy who went to night school
and had a cousin missing in New York.
The next day, two blocks down,
I was Carlos.
I held out my hand
and let the older men shake it,
stretched out my arm
and let the women fall against it.
They called me *sweet boy*.
I smelled their hair,
tasted their tears along my shoulder.

Possibility woke me early,
sent me prowling the shops downtown
for suits, a haircut, aftershave.
I pocketed my cash from the last two sales
and threw out the rest of the heroin.
Friday we stood on the corner,
brothers and sisters by the apartment sign,

my voice the baritone singing gospel
between the priest and the hockey boys.

Saturday night I sat in a high-rise
with the Sheraton beckoning outside the window,
a pale woman across the table
curved in a black dress
like an eclipse.

THE ARTIST

That second night, done with pacing the bedroom,
I sat sleepless on the end of the couch

at the Red Cross station, my fever high
and ears throbbing from an afternoon stooped

with Coltrane on headphones, awake two days
on coffee and Benzedrine and the same sick footage

on every channel. I couldn't stay inside.
I'd gone out seeking wounds, any sign of life

that I could hold in place and slip inside a frame.
Any proof that I had cared. My pencil ready,

I roamed past the stores with boarded windows,
the buzzing Korean signs, the houses

that melted into blocks with families gathered
at every table. Nothing beckoned me to stop.

But here at the station, everything cried out
to be captured: the weathered faces

five different shades of cream and coffee,
the priest with a biker slumped on each side,

the nurse's eyes red like a nightwatchman's
as she leaned the door open and cleared her throat

to choke out one more name. I steadied
my pad and waited. An old man rose

and limped past the boys, dusty like a scarecrow,
his shirt open to show a flag tattoo;

the girl wept beside them and groped blindly
for the tissues as they came around. At the end

of the couch, the one with the stroller laid pictures
of children on the table, two fingers twisted

and all nine gesturing, her voice cracked
telling stories of church and first words cooed

on her shoulder when Nana was out. As the minutes
passed, they huddled around her, the boys

on the carpet building Manhattan out of blocks,
the couples in their working clothes clutching

hands, bathed by lamps, until everything fused
into color, truth, a moment seared in time.

When the nurse stepped in and called my name,
I rolled up my sleeve and threw the pencil out.

THE NURSE'S DAUGHTER

You ask what I remember,
but I can say so little.
I was young.
I will share with you what comes back clearly,
and my parents will tell the rest.

The first few days were quiet time.
My father set games for me on the floor,
opened the drapes, read the news online.
One of the nights,
I spied on my mother
as she sat alone in the dark on the couch.
My father said not to disturb her,
and I did as I was told.

Saturday, she slept until noon.
Her white coat hung over the chair.
My father muttered, *Open heart yesterday,*
saying it was something nurses helped with,
then went to work, minding the jagged steps.

I played most of that day.
I had nothing else to do.
The doorbell rang twice, then fell silent;
my skirts faded out on the line.
When I dropped a glass, she appeared squint-eyed,
asking if anything was broken,
and left when I said I was all right.

Later, sitting up, she took a plastic blade
and a doll I hadn't touched in years
and showed me how to split a chest cleanly,
her thin fingers like a glove around mine.

THE EXPATRIATE

Tuesday night, I packed away the clothes,
tied the head scarf
in my gray sweat-lined dress
and rolled them at the back of the drawer.
I mouthed to myself, *It's time, it's time.*

He came home late, stroked my tangled hair,
asked me to reconsider.
I knew he would.
He liked me smooth,
loved the rounds of my head and shoulders
under the sleek protection of cotton,
the soft terrain spilling down to my feet
where his palms could play explorer.
I offered the newspaper,
pointed to the headlines
about *retribution* and *hate crimes against Muslims.*
He fought back tears.
The next morning, I went shopping alone
for jeans, a tank top, pepper spray.

He did not know
that I had lost my faith that summer,
that I had left my books to age on the shelf
and gone seeking God in tiny places.
Mischievous child, I savored the lifeguard
as he perched soldierlike over the pool,
the stray dogs barking at cars, the voices
sick with love on the passing radios,
the shouts of boys playing hockey in the street.

We slept without sheets, the electric fan broken.
I kissed my husband as he slept. I craved his person.
Before dawn, as the city loomed purple,
I slid to the balcony in his night shirt,
tossed my head back under the clouds
and played baptism in the rain.

Thursday morning, I cut my hair in the bathroom,
chugged brandy with the girls downstairs.
We called in sick at work.
They dusted a box
from the closet and threw in their hand-me-downs,
boy magazines, a pack of cigarettes.
Welcome to America, they told me.
Stretched on the carpet,
the TV turned to *COPS,*
we aimed guns with our fingers at the screen,
shouted *hands up, motherfucker,*
hit the pavement, jihadi pigs.

I staggered home at five, laughing, drunk for the first time.
He came in silently. My eyes tracked his shadow
as he undressed, shaved, murmured prayers alone.
In a vase,
I spread out the dozen roses
that a stranger had left on our doorstep,
tossed out the flier calling everyone
to rally for peace on the corner Friday.
He lay on the couch. I burned incense, waited,

then woke to an empty room,
his keys and wallet missing,
sun piercing the blinds. The rest of that week
I lived on the balcony, drink in hand
and watching the city turn gray, then neon,
not even budging when the mosque caught fire
Sunday night and my friends all called
leaving messages, praying I wasn't inside.

THE MORTICIAN

Evenings, we sat on the porch
and talked about the ones we'd embalmed
that afternoon.
They all looked too unknowing, too kind.
I read the statements,
the quotes from the family members buried
on page 10 of the morning paper,
remembering the white-haired woman
who let mosquitoes out the window,
the driller who used his rough, hard hands
to stroke cats in the sun.
The screen doors opened and neighbors passed by,
killers none of them — their eyes tried to say —
soft, smiling and articulate, a world away
from the person trapped in the weekend issue
in saturated color in that photograph.
But this was no painted work of art;
someone held that camera steady,
someone who would never dream
of holding a gun or scarring the faces
of the people that he'd just seen fall.
He clicked the flash and presses rolled
with his new assignment finished,
the truth the headlines couldn't tell
captured in a still-life scene.

Four days after Saturday morning,
I could still smell that magazine.

THE SEX OFFENDER

As time passed, I had grown to love them
the way all harmlessness turns to love.
I never stopped them for conversation.
They never offered their names.
But I memorized their movements:
how the Catholic mother hurried her children
past me in the courtyard,
how the man from Chicago looked the other way
when he stepped out in Cubs shirt for the newspaper.
The way he fingered his keys fetching mail
and watched me through the corner of his eye.

But you take me for a dangerous person.
I assure you I am not.
Watch my movements those days in September,
when the girls passed out prayer beads
and the neighbors gathered on the lawn.
Watch me dressing in my shirt and tie,
a consummate gentleman,
taking hugs from strangers.
Watch me holding the blind woman's hand
on the steps as she mourned the firefighters,
listening calmly like a dutiful son.

Then follow me Thursday, when I woke to the note
taped on every door, asking all the neighbors
to join hands on the lawn the following night
and sing for the dead. This from the girl
next door, the waitress. I knew her perfume.
I held it to the light, sniffed the *a*'s and *m*'s
drawn round like pregnant stomachs,
the heart floating over the single *i*.

But I did nothing wrong. I was one of them now.
The next night I shaved and dressed, carried the candle
she left on my porch to the crowd by the sidewalk.
They nodded and I nodded. I kept my hands in sight,
the way I had learned that night at the station.

The way I had trained myself to memorize.
Mark me there, my face lighted yellow,
shedding a tear like all the others.
Watch the flames dancing in a circle,
every last one part of the whole.

THE WAITRESS

you must understand
that that was ecstasy
the morning I woke ahead of the alarm
and prayed holy holy Jesus
in sweat kneeling by the single mattress
snatched my clothes and the bag of candles
I'd paid for with my tips that week
dressed to the sound
of the train hammering past
and slipped invisible
out the creaking screen door

the city around me sleeping
still and immaculate
the porch lights bronzing
the corners of American flags
I raced the sunrise
bent at each doorway
to fumble for matches in the cold
my fingers like a seamstress tearing tape
and posting the flier reading
WE ARE ALL PASSENGERS
breathing hard
I steadied a ballpoint
and scrawled a cross for each believer I knew
jotted peace signs for the strangers
Star of David for the Jews
a $20 bouquet of roses left
to coax out the couple from Iran

the bag once empty
I set the last one on the balcony
watched 30 candles burning
100 souls in each
the city's eye opening on railroad tracks
and televisions on all night in windows
my handiwork done

I slipped inside again
replaced the triple locks
and went back to sleep

that night I fell silent
like I always did
the youngest waitress on the late shift
serving beers to the men at the bar
the baseball game canceled
and their eyes tracking me instead
the break time I spent
sobbing in the bathroom
my fingers wrapped tight around the cross
begging to be His child again
begging for a glimmer of His light

then Friday evening
the neighbors came through shadows
holding the candles I'd left for them
families and stragglers approaching the spot
where the street lamp had died the week before
sweet procession of spirits
across a lightless field
like sinners to the river
like children to mother

and I was powerful that night
like I never was powerful again
my hand the conductor's baton
motioning them to stand in a circle
my voice the Pied Piper
calling for them to raise their candles
and shout *God bless America*
when the cars went by

all faces angelic now
no agnostics left
over the flicker of burning orange
the voices blending
elbows tight together

after another angry summer
up a flight of stairs
two blocks from the barrio
in a shabby complex
with half the air conditioners out

the man from the shop who trudged home cursing
with his tool box
now cradling his children
the veteran broken down in tears
and his wife in her flower dress helping him stand
the boys in their baggy shorts turned quiet
their stubble hair glistening
the lifeguard staring at the trees
hymns sounding over the crack of engines
by the light on the chipped apartment sign
the fence behind us curled like barb wire
no reason left for fear

THE LIFEGUARD

They asked me if I loved children.
I did not love children,
no more than the police loved the buskers
they chatted with on the curb every morning,
no more than the woman next door, the Christian,
loved the people she plied with prayer angels
from the bag around her shoulder.

I held my post five days a week
with my shades and towel, still as a scarecrow.
My life was service. I measured empathy in numbers.
One mouth sealed with another
filled two more lungs with air.
Two lungs opened two eyes
and set ten fingers trembling.
One break to the surface was another bed filled,
another future wife and mother sighing,
one fewer siren circling the block.

I pulled my last one out that Wednesday,
a boy about eleven.
He laid himself flat
at the bottom of the deep end,
hardened his stomach, then went limp
until I stretched him out on the concrete,
pumped his chest, locked his lips to mine.
Seven breaths and he coughed up water.
I held him steady. He broke loose and ran,
his feet out of rhythm lurching toward safety,
his hand groping for wherever was home.

The rest of that week, the pool empty,
I sat up the ladder tracking planes
as they crossed overhead again, bright as toys
and disappearing, screaming into the sky.
By Monday, the city looked painless below them,
the flags taken down along the block
and the flowers wilted by the school sign,

the cars by the curb with their painted slogans
chipped in the sun, the drippings of candles.
The whole street stood without a visible scar.
I lost interest in what I owned
and headed off to enlist.

IV.

THE DESERT

When it ends the road slips back into what it always was,
A mirror for the rider to find himself within.

—Paul Kareem Tayyar

GHOST TOWN PANTOUM

In the ghost town, we walk hand in hand,
thin shadows waving over lost saloons
and the ragged posters of medicine shows,
our watches hidden, forgetting time.

Thin shadows waving over lost saloons,
we guess at the names on the faded headstones.
Our watches hidden, forgetting time,
we kiss in the shade of the jail. She tells me

we guess at the names on the faded headstones
as we walk on our own crooked journey;
we kiss in the shade of the jail. She tells me
stories plied from the gospel wagon

as we walk on our own crooked journey.
Her voice is shadow now; the light rays expand.
Stories plied from the gospel wagon
fade on a prayer book's tattered pages.

Her voice is shadow now; the light rays expand
past lovemaking stains on single beds,
fade on a prayer book's tattered pages.
The chapel towers over sunburned land.

Past lovemaking stains on single beds
and the ragged posters of medicine shows,
the chapel towers over sunburned land.
In the ghost town, we walk hand in hand.

JANUARY

(I know) I'm losing you
we speak
the words in parentheses
never raising our voices enough
to rattle the ice
on the locked windows
a newspaper lies
with its secrets open
around the plates on the kitchen table
the last stains of yesterday's meals
left drying
in sunbeams
your sweat still clings
to the aging mattress
the nights that we lie awake together
your breaths thin
arms aromatic
with the hot musk of secondhand coats
sometimes I watch you
(you must know this)
naked inside the morning mirror
chest hanging casually
eyes tracking patterns
in the gray hair swirling
between your fingers
(I remember the sweat lines
the stifled laughs
shivering up the stairs in winter
two waists entwined on a couch
red-eyed
the floor scattered with a younger man's shoes)
we live
in solitudes
smile across them
pack universes in our drawers
wake at dawn
to the roar of engines

pounding a new day
through the rush of snow
only
those moments in the evening
when the sky pulls low
you lean against me
wrap your fingers
around the hands
that brushed the makeup off your cheeks
murmur the words
you heard last night
in dreams about ascending
(lights blinding
I know)

EVERYONE FACES THE DAWN ALONE

Everyone faces the dawn alone
after they've walked together at night,
huddled closely, braced for the moment
when they'll stand under a cold white sun

and the long shadows behind their backs
will stretch out in the morning light
over the tracks of men and women
coming to their own roads' end,

where consciousness comes in a flush of pain
but leaves all the senses awake at last.
A loved one smiles from far away
and becomes a stranger once again,

as houses turn back into shelters,
and voices turn back into sounds,
and rooms turn back into four thin walls
with a roof that couldn't stay on.

SANTA ANA

This morning I drove through Santa Ana
with trumpets playing on the radio,
half awake and hearing the music
loud and fast
and running up and down the scale
like notes flying on a merry-go-round,
until the buildings started to rise
and fall,
and the red graffiti on the walls
fused together into valentines,
and voices started drifting out
and reading the names on every sign,
and everyone on the sidewalk
fell in perfect step together,
taller faster and younger
than they'd been before the day began,
and over on Main and 1st St.,
with my foot up off the pedal,
I watched a girl riding by me
with sparklers in the wheels of her
bicycle, shooting colors on the pavement
like every light inside a rainbow
rolled up in a paper stick
and finally set on fire.

This evening, when the streets are still
and the colors have faded back to grey,
I want to be the last one standing
out on the corner of Main and 1st,
sweeping up the trails of ashes
that she left behind.

TESTAMENT

Let the band play ragged when they lay me to rest,
seven bent trumpets shuffling out of time
on a parched gray field, jagged red weeds
cutting cartwheels through the twisting valley,
a procession missing shoes. Let the drummers
pound out rhythms with the flats of their palms,
drumsticks forgotten, amazed one more time
by the instant pulse of a hand on parchment.
Let the singers warble, ten happy travelers
drunk from the mornings after drunken wakes,
chasing through melodies, red-faced, laughing
when their voices strike in spontaneous harmony.
Where the hillside ends, let them lose formation,
the conductor limping on his thin baton
over skulls and monuments, the silver harmonicas
shaking a field of polished headstones,
two dozen marches stumbling through sharp grass,
each note triumphant and out of tune.

CHASE

When we walk along the beach
with the moon out of sight,
we can't even measure the steps that we take;
long sand dunes hidden in shadows
rise and fall underneath our feet
as you pass laughing over the hill
and feel the salt air stinging your face.
I trudge after you like a blind man
with his legs about to go,
but strong enough to make it over
that last slope before the sea,
following the voice I once heard
inside my head,
and, when I catch you out in the tide,
will never have to chase again.

DESERT HIGHWAY, NEW YEAR'S EVE

A quiet brush of the apocalypse,
a splash of orange behind the low clouds
bathes her skin as she steps down the canyon,
echoes muffled underneath her soles.

A sandstorm is coming and the desert waits
to grow tighter in the bleeding dusk,
the short trees to bend, invisible currents
to churn dust from the mouths of craters.

He sits on the ledge, too distant to hear her,
her coat in his lap. The chrome of their wheels
rusts to brown in the canceling shadows,
the tire treads scratching a wavering road.

He swallows, rubs the sweat on her collar
as she sinks away from him down the valley,
watches the muscles flex in her shoulders
and push back the cold. *I just need a walk,*

she whispered to him. *Can you stay behind
and guard the camper?* She stretches now,
displays the arms that carried her luggage
when they took to the motels in August,

the legs that hardened standing in line
for pills, bail bonds, loans. As she bends
to tear a rose from the brush, he feels
his tattoos burn again, mouths the words

he tried that morning when she stood at the window
and dreamed out loud about a silent world
without alarms or sirens, the men deserted
from the bars she worked in every other city,

her car disappearing in a white garage
on a street of houses blending together,

a picket fence and a lawn. She ascends
the valley again, slides her own door open,

wraps the coat back around her shoulders.
They drive and the clouds sink lower. That night,
as she lies face down on motel pillows,
he pictures her walking alone again

through the desert, the only figure left moving
in a shattered landscape of brush and bone
as if God had set creation backward,
let the footsteps perish one at a time

and left her to explore, her arms
relaxed at last in the arid evening,
her skirt gliding around unfinished roots
and coyotes fallen in ravines. Like a child,

she slides off her shoes, extends a finger
to brush the inescapable veins
of a perfect leaf, the infinite patterns
of snakeskin impaled on a jagged stone,

then dances, weightless, across the canyon,
her fists high, spinning in orange glow
as the world lies back and waits to pass under
when the last pair of eyes is closed.

BLUES MAN

One century (which time let go)
lives on stubbornly in this room.
The speakers hum with tales
of Sunday gospel, police dogs on the shoals,
bootleg whiskey at the back of a bus
in Chicago after the war.
Thirty chairs and a light turned low
give shelter from the cold outside
where the word 'legend' is scrawled in black
by the photograph on the window.
Hoarse, white-haired, he squints at the figures
who watch him back from the crooked tables,
his fingers conjuring the notes from childhood,
his foot on the case tapping rhymes.

You're healed now, say the thin girl's eyes.
I'm out of change, says the man with the jar.
A couple sways in the dark by the counter;
the boys sit up front, eager, taking notes down.

Their pens sustain him. At ten, alone,
he walks by the ghosts of a college town,
the bootleggers painted solemn on
the gallery walls, Chicago beamed
into the multiplex, the gnash of police dogs
pantomimed through a flickering reel,
the bus stopping by the curb to take him
to his next one-night stand, the headlights gold
as the waitress shuts out the light,
unscarred,
and heads for the dead of home.